WHAT A
WONDERFUL
WORD

For Stu, who I love beyond words
~ Nicola Edwards

To my parents, who were always there for me
~ Luisa Uribe

First American Edition 2018
Kane Miller, A Division of EDC Publishing

Text by Nicola Edwards
Text copyright © Caterpillar Books 2018
Illustration copyright © Luisa Uribe 2018
First published in Great Britain 2018 by 360 Degrees,
an imprint of the Little Tiger Group.

For information contact:
Kane Miller, A Division of EDC Publishing
P.O. Box 470663
Tulsa, OK 74147-0663

www.kanemiller.com
www.edcpub.com
www.usbornebooksandmore.com

Library of Congress Control Number: 2017942237

Printed and bound in China
CPB/1400/0661/0917
10 9 8 7 6 5 4 3 2 1
ISBN: 978-1-61067-722-6

WHAT A WONDERFUL WORD

Kane Miller
A DIVISION OF EDC PUBLISHING

Written by Nicola Edwards
Illustrated by Luisa Uribe

CONTENTS

INTRODUCTION

You might wonder, as you open this book, how you can have a collection of untranslatable words and give translations for them. Is there any word from any language that is really untranslatable? Maybe, maybe not. But whereas the English word "blue" becomes "azul" in Spanish, "mavi" in Turkish, "àwö sánmà" in Yoruba, and so on, some words just don't have simple one-word translations.

Sometimes this is because the words are tied to a specific way of life. You probably won't often be searching for something in the water using only your feet if you live in a New York City apartment, for example! On the other hand, an untranslatable word might be just the thing to describe something we're all familiar with. Who hasn't had to move scalding-hot food around their mouth in an attempt to cool it down enough to eat it? Why don't we all have a word for that? Who knows? But isn't it wonderful that, somewhere in the world, one exists?

Untranslatable words, then, are great examples of how beautiful language can be. It can always surprise us and teach us new things about ourselves, each other, and the world. It tells us what an interesting mix human beings are, and it reassures us that we are understood, that we're all the same on some level. It's nice, isn't it, to know that someone else has had the same feeling or experience as you, and given it, at long last, a name of its own?

GÖKOTTA

Swedish

To wake up early in the morning so you can go outside to hear the first birds singing

Gökotta literally means "early cuckoo morning." On Ascension Day (apparently the best time of year to hear the cuckoo's call), it's traditional for Swedes to go out first thing to hear these birds sing, and perhaps even enjoy a picnic in the fresh air.

In the depths of winter, in some northern parts of Sweden above the Arctic Circle, you might get as little as three hours of sunlight per day, so Swedes really appreciate the long daylight hours of the summer months.

Sweden is a country of beautiful scenery, and its people want to keep it that way. Only 1% of waste in Sweden ends up in landfills — the rest is recycled or converted into energy!

Less than 3% of the land mass of Sweden has been developed, and forests cover 69% of the country.

VERSCHLIMMBESSERUNG

German

A supposed improvement that makes things worse

The *verschlimmbesserung* is universal. In 2012 an elderly Spanish woman caused a global media sensation when she tried to repair damage to a nineteenth-century fresco and made a pretty spectacular mess of it. The "repaired" image of Jesus was dubbed "Ecce Mono" (Behold the Monkey), and tourists began to flock to the church, tickled by the thought of seeing the woman's "handiwork."

In 1896, German inventor Martin Goetze was granted a patent for a dimple-making machine. In the quest for dimpled cuteness, Goetze's machine used a crank connected to two revolving metal arms with knobs at the ends, which would basically squeeze indentations into the skin. Ouch!

Despite the occasional questionable "improvement," Germans have also invented a lot of pretty amazing things, like aspirin, the car, Christmas trees, the helicopter and X-rays.

GLUGGAVEÐUR

Icelandic

Weather that looks beautiful while you're inside, but is much too cold when you step outside

This word literally means "window weather" because it is best enjoyed inside the house.

All that window weather has created a nation of writers and bookworms. Iceland has more writers, more books published, and more books read, per capita, than anywhere else in the world.

An amazing 10% of Icelanders will publish a book in their lifetime!

KOYAANISQATSI

— Hopi —

Nature that is out of balance or a way of life that is so crazy it cannot continue long-term

The Hopi people are Native Americans who have lived in Arizona for thousands of years. The word "Hopi" is said to mean "peaceful ones," and Hopi culture teaches the importance of human harmony with nature.

The Montana Glacier National Park in the USA has only 25 glaciers left from the 150 that existed in 1910. As glaciers like this melt, sea levels rise, causing more and more floods, which especially affect coastal areas.

Around 18% of the world's greenhouse gases (which cause global warming) are produced by livestock. That's more than cars, planes, and all other forms of transportation combined. So consuming less meat and fewer animal products can help us rebalance nature.

PORONKUSEMA

Finnish

The distance a reindeer can walk before needing to use the bathroom

14

A *poronkusema* is a traditional measure of distance in the Finnish countryside. It's not very precise but is apparently no more than 4.7 miles long.

To the Sami people of northern Finland, reindeer are so important that they have around 400 words for the food, tools, and other products they get from the animal.

Reindeer have an amazing sense of smell. They can sniff out food even when it's buried under more than 20 inches of snow.

A reindeer's eyes change color with the seasons! They go from a yellow-green in the summer to a deep blue in the dark winter. This color change scatters the incoming light and helps the reindeer to see better!

4.7 miles to JUUJARVI

KAZURI

Swahili

Small and beautiful

The small and beautiful red-cheeked cordon-bleu is a tiny finch, around 5 inches long. Male and female finches look similar, but only males have the distinctive rosy cheeks.

This bird is a common sight across central and eastern Africa, including southern Tanzania.

Tanzania's mpingo trees take more than 70 years to reach maturity and produce the world's most expensive wood.

The mpingo tree is known as the "music tree of Africa." Its wood has a beautiful sound quality that is ideal for making musical instruments.

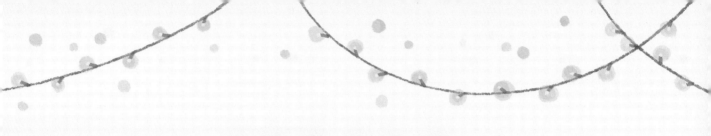

TARTLE

Scots

To hesitate because you have forgotten someone's name

The most common Scottish surnames (in order) are Smith, Brown, and Wilson, and one in every eight last names begins with Mac or Mc, so these might be good guesses if you find yourself tartling in Scotland!

Why is remembering names so tricky? It could be the "next-in-line" effect, where people rehearse introducing themselves at the expense of listening to the person who's speaking.

Another issue with remembering names is that they're random and don't give us any useful information about a person. (You can't tell that a Dave is a Dave just by looking at him!) Our brains tend to retain information better when it's connected to other information. That's why a common memory trick is to connect a name to a color or to remember Dave as "Dave, Denise's son, from Dumfries."

Scientists estimate that the human brain has a memory capacity of 2.5 million gigabytes — that's the equivalent of about three million hours of TV!

FRIOLERO

Spanish

Someone who is always cold

Spain is the sunniest country in Europe and its Mediterranean coastline gets, on average, more than 300 days of sunshine every year.

Despite its warm and sunny reputation, Spain has three different climate zones, due to its large size. It is even possible to ski in the mountains there!

Spain has over 4,970 miles of beaches, which are popular with locals and tourists alike.

MURR-MA

—— Wagiman ——

To walk through the water, searching for something with only your feet

The Wagiman language is native to Australia's Northern Territory. There are only a few people left who speak Wagiman, and as most of them are elderly, the language is unlikely to survive much longer.

A special prosthetic limb called a "Murr-ma" has been created by scientists to help amputees go from running on the sand to swimming in the sea. It looks a little like a futuristic fish fin!

JUGAAD

Hindi

The ability to get by without lots of resources, and find new and creative ways of solving a problem

In Indian culture, it is considered important to establish harmony between yourself and the universe and to make peace with chaos and difficulty. The idea of making the best of things is deep-rooted.

75% of Indians earn less than $80 a month, so many people have to be creative and resourceful to make ends meet.

India's recycling industry employs more than a million people. For example, as many as 8,500 mobile phones are dismantled in Delhi every day for reuse of their parts and materials.

With 356 million people between the ages of 10 and 24, India has the world's largest youth population. It's not surprising that the country has so many clever and exciting new ideas!

GOBBLEDYGOOK

English

Text or speech that contains a lot of complicated jargon

The word *gobbledygook* was coined by Fontaine Maury Maverick, a Texas politician, in 1944. He used it in a memo during World War II, asking people to use plain, simple English when they interacted.

Maverick's inspiration for this useful word was the noise a turkey makes, "always gobbledygobbling and strutting with ridiculous pomposity."

English has more words than any other language in the world (around 250,000 altogether), so there are many options if you want to speak gobbledygook!

26

RETROUVAILLES

French

The happiness of being reunited with someone after a long time apart

Gare du Nord in Paris is the busiest train station in Europe. Some 190 million travelers pass through it every year.

The iris, or *fleur-de-lis*, is France's national flower. Its three petals are supposed to symbolize faith, wisdom, and chivalry.

NAKAMA

---- Japanese ----

Friends who are like family

The ideas of *soto* (outside) and *uchi* (inside) are very important social concepts in Japan. Becoming *nakama* or working your way up from *soto* to *uchi* takes a long time and involves a lot of give and take.

The traditional form of greeting in Japan is a bow. The lower you bow, the more respect you are showing.

Japan has more elderly people than anywhere else in the world, with over 26% of the population older than 65. Elderly people are highly respected in Japan and at mealtimes are served their food and drink first.

Japan has 5.6 million vending machines on its streets, selling everything from cooked pizza to underwear to raw eggs!

MENCOLEK

---- Indonesian ----

The act of tapping someone lightly on the opposite shoulder from behind to fool them

Indonesia has more than 76 million children. That's the fourth-largest child population in the world.

Komodo dragons, the largest lizards in the world, are found in the wild only in Indonesia. They can eat 80% of their body weight in a single meal!

As recently as the 1960s, 80% of Indonesia was covered in forest. Sadly, 72% of its ancient forest has now been lost because of global demand for paper and palm oil.

ABBIOCCO

Italian

Drowsiness from eating a big meal

Pasta has been eaten in Italy in one form or another since 400 BCE.

When McDonald's first opened in Rome in 1986, protesters gave away free spaghetti outside to remind potential customers that "better" food was available to them elsewhere in the city!

The world's most expensive pizza costs more than $8,800 and is made by Italian chef Renato Viola. Its luxurious toppings include three types of caviar, lobster, and hand-picked grains of pink sea salt. It takes a whopping 72 hours to make!

ISHQ

Arabic

A perfect love without jealousy or inconsistency that holds two people together

In Morocco, it is the liver that is traditionally considered the symbol of love, not the heart!

Scientists have found that long-term couples with deep, strong connections can ease each other's pain in stressful and unpleasant situations simply by holding hands.

The Harvard Grant study, which began in 1938, has found that there are two pillars of happiness. One of these is love and the other is "finding a way of coping with life that does not push love away."

SHLIMAZL

Yiddish

A person who suffers from relentless bad luck

It is a Yiddish custom to spit three times or say "pu pu pu" when you've spoken about something that is going well (just like English speakers "knock on wood"). This is meant to ward off the evil eye and prevent the tempting of fate.

It is also customary to chew on a piece of thread if someone is sewing your clothes as you wear them. This may have to do with the fact that shrouds are sewn around the dead; the act of chewing shows that you're still alive!

TALAKA

— Belarusian —

The act of working cooperatively, as when assisting someone in his or her house or field without expecting payment other than a good meal shared at the end of the day

Belarusians seem to love potatoes. The average person eats almost 400 pounds of potatoes per year. That's the highest level of potato consumption in the world!

Birch sap is a popular drink in Belarus — and there's plenty of it around, as 42% of Belarus is forest!

The *draniki* (potato pancake) is the national dish of Belarus. Other popular meals include *machanka* (pork stew), *kletski* (stuffed dumplings), and *babka* (grated potato pie).

PÅLEGG

Norwegian

Anything and everything you can put on a slice of bread

Many Norwegians love an open-faced sandwich or *smørbrød* (pronounced "smurrbrur"). Rye bread is often used as the base, and popular toppings include smoked salmon, shrimp, cheese, egg, bacon, liver pâté, meatballs, cucumber, and the national staple, herring (but not usually all together!).

It was a Norwegian carpenter, Thor Bjørklund, who invented the cheese slicer in 1925. It was based on a carpenter's planing tool and is also useful for slicing cucumbers for your *smørbrød*!

A popular cheese for topping *smørbrød* in Norway is *brunost*, a caramelized whey cheese that tastes similar to fudge! Many Norwegians love it, but visitors to the country are often less convinced of its deliciousness.

PROMAJA

The much-hated draft created by wind
blowing between two open windows

People in the Balkans, particularly older people, dread *promaja*. It is blamed for various illnesses such as numbness, colds, muscle stiffness, and headaches, as well as more serious complaints.

Anyone who worries about *promaja* should perhaps be glad they don't live on the desolate Kerguelen Islands in the Indian Ocean. As winds here often reach 93 miles per hour, local butterflies have evolved to be wingless, to avoid being blown out to sea!

Even this is nothing compared to the winds on Saturn, which can reach speeds of over 1,118 miles per hour and are the strongest in the solar system.

CAFUNÉ

— Brazilian Portuguese —

The act of running your fingers through someone's hair

Brazil has more species of monkey than any other nation on Earth. For monkeys, as for humans, hair grooming is a kind of social bonding.

Capuchin monkeys are both intelligent and small, usually 12-22 inches long, which can make them skillful little thieves!

They were the first non-ape primates to be observed using tools in the wild, and in 2005, a Yale University psychologist and economist even taught capuchins how to use money!

MISTIMANCHACHI

Quechua

A light drizzle that frightens city dwellers,
fashionable people, and tourists

The people who speak Quechua are native to the Andean region of South America, which includes the mountains of Peru, Bolivia, and Ecuador. These people are mostly rural and are more likely to welcome rain than visitors as rain provides much-needed water for their crops and animals.

In the town of Tarata, in Bolivia, at the annual San Severino festival, people joyfully celebrate the coming of the November rain.

PELINTI

Buli

To move food that is too hot around your mouth as you wait for it to cool down

Red Red is a popular dish in Ghana, where Buli is spoken. It is a black-eyed-pea stew made with palm oil (which gives the meal its red coloring). It is often served with fried plantains.

Jollof rice is another much-loved dish in Ghana, and this spicy favorite is now popular around the world. It is often eaten with chicken, but there are many variations.

In many parts of the world, it is very bad manners to use your left hand when eating, because this is the "unclean" hand used in the bathroom. If you try to hail a cab in Ghana using your left hand, drivers will not stop for you!

HIRAETH

Welsh

Nostalgic longing for a homeland or past

Wales is a country steeped in history. It is the land of the legendary King Arthur and has more castles per square mile than any other country in the world.

A 2011 census showed that only 19% of Welsh people could speak Welsh, but there have been efforts to promote the language to prevent it from dying out and to keep this part of Welsh culture alive.

A surprising stronghold of the Welsh language can be found in Patagonia. Welsh speakers who settled here over 150 years ago thought the Chubut province's remote location would ensure the language's survival — and indeed there are still some 5,000 Welsh speakers living there!

WHIMSY

English

Playfully quaint or fanciful behavior or humor

The World Worm Charming Championship started in 1980 in Cheshire, England, and is now an annual event where competitors try to coax as many worms as possible from their 10-by-10-foot patch of grass in 30 minutes.

There are 18 rules for the event, one of which is that "Competitors who do not wish to handle worms can appoint another person, called a 'Gillie,' to do it for them."

There is an International Federation of Charming Worms and Allied Pastimes (IFCWAP), which also deals with unusual sports like underwater ludo and ice tiddlywinks.

The UK has many other whimsical annual events — like the Cooper's Hill cheese-rolling contest and a bog-snorkeling triathlon in Wales!

POCHEMUCHKA

Russian

*A child who asks "why?" all the time; a person
who asks too many questions*

Back in 1939, Winston Churchill memorably described Russia as "a riddle wrapped in a mystery inside an enigma."

In 2007, Aleksandr Kuzmin, the mayor of the Siberian town of Megion, banned officials from making excuses. Among the 27 phrases he banned was, "I don't know!"

"Closed" or "forbidden" cities appeared in Russia in the 1940s, and some still exist today. They do not appear on maps, mail cannot be delivered there, and their walls are heavily guarded. No foreigners are admitted, and even Russians, unless they have a special pass to visit close family members, are not allowed in.

NAM JAI

A spirit of selfless generosity and kindness; a willingness to make sacrifices for friends and extend hospitality to strangers

Thailand is known as the "Land of Smiles" and is world famous for its wonderful hospitality.

The Thai capital, Bangkok, was the most-visited city in the world in 2016, with more than 21 million international guests.

One of Thailand's most charming festivals is the Monkey Buffet in Lopburi province, where locals give thanks to the village monkeys for bringing thousands of tourists there each year. Some 600 monkeys are invited, and the generous banquet includes fresh fruit, more than two tons of grilled sausages, and ice cream!

KAWAAKARI

— Japanese —

The gleam of last light on a river's surface at dusk

The first climber of Japan's Mount Fuji is thought to have been a monk in 663 CE. The mountain was forbidden to female visitors until 1868.

Mount Fuji is actually three separate volcanoes, one on top of the other. The bottom layer is the Komitake volcano, then the Kofuji volcano, then Shin-Fuji, which is the youngest of the three.

In Shinto mythology, the goddess of the Sun, Amaterasu, quarreled with her brother Tsukuyomi, the god of the Moon, when he killed the food goddess, Uke Mochi, for vomiting! After that, Amaterasu never wanted to see him again, and that is how day got separated from night!

KALPA

Sanskrit

An unimaginably long period of time

Perhaps it's no surprise that this word exists in Sanskrit, which at 6,000 years old is one of the oldest languages in the world. It's said that 97% of the world's languages have been influenced by Sanskrit in some way.

Although impressively old by human standards, Sanskrit is a newborn compared to our stars, which live for millions to trillions of years, depending on their size.

A *kalpa* is a period of time that is said to last long enough for the universe to experience a complete cycle of creation and destruction.

Apparently, when Buddha was asked how long a *kalpa* was, he replied that it was the length of time it would take for a stone, 16 miles on each side, to be worn away if touched with a cloth every 100 years!

A WORD ABOUT PRONUNCIATION

We have included a rough guide to pronunciation in this book so you can enjoy trying the words out yourself. However, explaining pronunciation in writing can be tricky, especially for tonal languages (like Buli) where the pitch of your voice is important and can change the meaning of your words completely! So please remember that the phonetic spellings we have supplied are for general guidance only.

With sincere thanks to Dr Soe-Tjen Marching at the School of Oriental and African Studies; George Akanlig-Pare at the University of Ghana; Milli Spence and Emily Stuyvers at Sustainable Bolivia; Hipólito Peralta Ccama at the Ministry of Education, Peru; Anthony Filmer and Rayna Popova.